History *of* Britain

The Spanish Armada

Brian Williams

Illustrated by Mark Bergin

HAMLYN

HISTORY OF BRITAIN – THE SPANISH ARMADA
was produced for Hamlyn Children's Books
by Lionheart Books, London

Editor: Lionel Bender
Designer: Ben White
Editorial Assistant: Madeleine Samuel
Picture Researcher: Jennie Karrach
Media Conversion and Typesetting:
  Peter MacDonald

Educational Consultant: Jane Shuter
Editorial Advisors: Andrew Farrow, Paul Shuter

Production Controller: Christine Campbell
Editorial Director: David Riley

First published in Great Britain in 1995
by Hamlyn International Books,
an imprint of Reed Children's Books,
Michelin House, 81 Fulham Road, London SW3 6RB,
and Auckland, Melbourne, Singapore and Toronto.

Copyright © 1995 Reed International Books Limited

ISBN 0 600 58603 0 Hb
ISBN 0 600 58604 9 Pb

British Library Cataloguing-in-Publication Data
A catalogue record for this book is available
from the British Library.

Printed in Italy

Acknowledgements
All artwork by Mark Bergin
All maps by Hayward Art Group.

Photo credits
The Mansell Collection: pages 5 (centre), 7 (left, right), 12 (top), 13 (top).
By kind permission of the Marquess of Tavistock and the Trustees of the
Bedford Estate: pages 4, 20. National Maritime Museum, London: pages 6
(top), 12 (bottom), 14, 16 (left). National Portrait Gallery, London: pages 5
(top), 22 (bottom). Fotomas Index: pages 6 (bottom), 11, 15 (bottom,
centre left), 16 (right), 17 (bottom), 18 (top), 19 (top). Scottish National
Portrait Gallery: page 6 (bottom). Weidenfeld and Nicholson Archive/Museo
Naval, Madrid: page 8 (top). Archivo General de Simancas/Foto Cacho:
page 8 (bottom left). The Master and Fellows, Magdalene College,
Cambridge: page 10 (top, bottom). Plymouth City Museum and Art Gallery
Collection: page 15 (top). Ulster Museum: pages 16 (top), 20-21. Colin
Martin: pages 19 (bottom), 21 (centre). Michael Holford: pages 18-19.
Tiroler Landesmuseum Ferdinandeum, Innsbruck: page 17 (top). National
Trust Photographic Library: page 22 (top).

Cover: Main illustration by Mark Bergin, icon artwork by Jonathan Adams.
Photo credits: Drake and circumnavigation, Fireships – The Mansell
Collection. Elizabeth I – National Portrait Gallery, London. Armada map –
National Maritime Museum, London. Designing ships – Master and Fellows,
Magdalene College, Cambridge.

PLACES TO VISIT

Here are some museums and sites which contain exhibits
about the Armada. Your local tourist office will be able to tell
you about places to visit in your area.

Berkeley Castle, Gloucestershire. Drake's wooden chest,
from the *Golden Hind.*

Buckland Abbey, Devon. Home of Grenville and Drake, now
a museum; has banners flown on board the *Golden Hind.*

Burghley House, Huntingdon. Home of William Cecil, Lord
Burghley, minister to Elizabeth.

City Museum and Art Gallery, Plymouth, Devon. Has
Drake's Cup and a portrait of Hawkins.

Deal Castle, Kent. Coastal fortification, built 1539-40 to
defend against enemy ships.

Longleat, Wiltshire. Great Elizabethan House, begun in 1568.

Museum of Artillery, Woolwich, London. Has early guns.
Woolwich is the site of a former naval dockyard.

National Maritime Museum, Greenwich, London. Has
pictures, models, maps, and items from ships of the
1500s.

National Portrait Gallery, London. Has pictures of Howard,
Drake and other Elizabethans.

Penshurst Place, Kent. Birthplace of soldier and writer Sir
Philip Sidney (1554-1586).

Portsmouth, Hampshire. Pre-Armada Tudor warship *Mary
Rose*, raised from seabed and restored.

**Scottish National Portrait Gallery and National Museum
of Antiquities**, Edinburgh. Has pictures and relics of Mary,
Queen of Scots.

Shetland County Museum, Lerwick, Shetland Islands. Finds
from Armada wrecks.

Southsea Castle, Hampshire. Built in 1546 against sea
invasion.

St Faith's Church, King's Lynn, Norfolk. Picture of Queen
Elizabeth at Tilbury.

Tavistock, Devon. Drake's birthplace, with a statue.

Tower of London has Elizabethan armour and weapons.

Victoria and Albert Museum, London, has the Armada jewel
presented to Sir Thomas Heneage by Queen Elizabeth.

Ulster Museum, Belfast. Has finds from Armada wrecks.

INTRODUCTION

In 1588 King Philip II of Spain sent a fleet of armed ships, or Armada, to attack England. Philip believed victory in battle would end his quarrel with England's Queen Elizabeth I, and bring peace to Europe.

Part of Spain's quarrel with England was over religion. Most people in Europe were Christians but they were divided between Catholics and Protestants. Catholics accepted the Pope, in Rome, as their religious leader. Protestants did not. Spain was a powerful Catholic country, at war with the Protestant Dutch for rule of their land. England's queen was Protestant and so were most English people. By invading England, Philip hoped to make the country Catholic again.

CONTENTS

REASONS FOR WAR

"She has seized the kingdom, and monstrously taken over as Head of the Church", the Pope said of Elizabeth I. This gave Philip II of Spain a reason for war, and a chance to take revenge for raids on Spanish ships by English pirates.

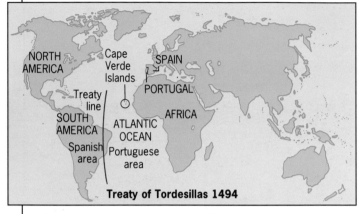

Treaty of Tordesillas 1494

△ **Spain claimed most of the American New World**, and allowed no rivals. The Spanish killed French settlers in Florida, and barred foreign traders from their colonies. The English defied the ban.

▷ **Philip of Spain and Mary Tudor.** Mary wanted a son, who would rule a Catholic England and Spain. But she died childless. Her Protestant half-sister, Elizabeth, became queen.

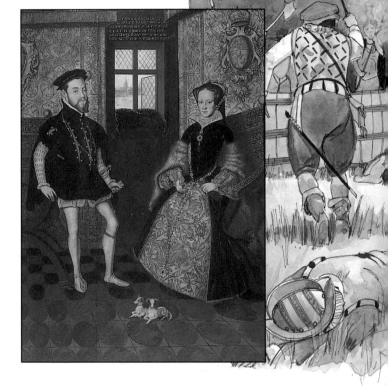

The religious quarrel was an old one. Elizabeth's father, King Henry VIII, had broken with the Catholic Church. In 1527 he asked the Pope (the head of the Church) for a divorce from his Spanish wife, Catherine of Aragon. The Pope refused. So in 1534 Henry made himself head of the Church in England, divorced Catherine and married Anne Boleyn, a Protestant. Catholics did not accept the divorce and new marriage as lawful.

Henry died in 1549. His son, Edward, a Protestant, became king but died in 1553. Then Edward's sister, Mary Tudor, became queen. Her mother was the divorced Catherine. Mary set out to make England Catholic again, and in 1554 she married Prince Philip of Spain.

In 1556 Philip became king of Spain, the strongest nation in Europe. He ruled the Low Countries (Belgium and the Netherlands) as well as Spain and, when Mary died in 1558, Philip hoped to keep control over England too. He wanted to marry Mary's sister, Elizabeth, England's new queen, but she refused. She also let England become Protestant again. This angered Philip.

In the 1560s English ships began to raid Spanish fleets returning from America with gold. Elizabeth feared Philip's anger about this. Also, she knew that some English Catholics were plotting to replace her as queen with her Catholic cousin, Mary, Queen of Scots (Scotland was a separate country). The English government believed Spain backed such plots.

England had no strong allies. France was split by religious wars. The Dutch Protestants were losing their revolt against Spanish control of the Low Countries. In 1579 Spain tried to start an uprising in Ireland against English rule. It failed, but Spain would try again.

◁ **Sir Francis Drake (left) was England's most feared sea captain.** He sailed round the world (1577-80), seeking Spanish treasure. In 1586 Drake and his soldiers looted the Spanish city of Cartagena (in modern Colombia). The Spanish blamed Queen Elizabeth (above) for backing such raids, and taking her share of the profits.

▷ **Catholics and Protestants in England distrusted one another.**
● The Catholic Church thought Protestants were heretics, or unbelievers.
● In Elizabeth's Protestant England, Catholics were accused of spying and treason.
● 'Scare-stories' reached England of Protestants tortured by the Spanish Inquisition, the religious 'police'.

INVASION FEARS

"In the whole realm there are but two fortresses which stand a three days' siege". An English Catholic priest in exile in Spain told King Philip that England would soon fall to a Spanish invasion. Philip ordered his commanders to assemble a great fleet, or Armada.

▷ **England's land defences were weak.** Some coastal forts had cannon. But the army was small and unlikely to stop experienced Spanish troops.

Spain and England moved towards war when in 1585 Elizabeth sent an army to help Dutch Protestants fight the Spanish.

Early in 1586, Philip finalized plans for the invasion of England. The Duke of Parma's army in the Netherlands would cross to England in barges, march on London, and force Elizabeth to plead for mercy. To protect Parma's ships across the Channel and to carry weapons and equipment needed for the land battle, an Armada would be sent from Spain. This fleet was to be led by the Marquis of Santa Cruz and would carry an extra 20,000 soldiers to help Parma's forces.

In August 1586, Sir Francis Walsingham, England's spy-catcher, uncovered another plot to murder Elizabeth. Her cousin, Mary Stuart, Queen of Scots, was an exile in England. Mary was charged with taking part in the plot, and put to death.

In April 1587, Drake attacked the Spanish port of Cadiz. He destroyed ships and stores meant for the Armada. Downcast, Philip became ill. The invasion had to be put off.

▽ **The Spanish navy** had shown its skills in the defeat of the Turks at Lepanto (near Greece) in 1571 (below). But England's navy was to prove its equal.

▷ **Mary, Queen of Scots, in 1578.** Mary had lived in England since 1567, and was a threat to Elizabeth. Had the childless Elizabeth died, Catholic Mary would have been queen of England. Her son, James, was next in line to be England's king. Mary was executed in 1587.

△ **Sir Francis Walsingham** was England's Secretary of State, in charge of foreign affairs. His secret agents uncovered plots against Queen Elizabeth.

△ **Alessandro Farnese, Duke of Parma**, was governor of the Netherlands. He had fought at Lepanto, and now led Spain's army against the Dutch rebels.

◁ **At forts such as Deal Castle in Kent**, built by Henry VIII for defence against a French invasion, gunners and pikemen made ready to fight the Spanish.

The Spanish Navy

Early in 1588, the Marquis of Santa Cruz, the Armada's mastermind, died. Philip chose the Duke of Medina Sidonia to take his place. "Sir, I have not health for the sea, for I know by the small experience that I have had afloat that I soon become seasick." Medina Sidonia was not eager to lead the fleet.

By the spring of 1588, Philip was well again. He worked tirelessly at studying maps and giving orders, certain that God would grant the Armada victory. Government officials rode from village to village in Spain, collecting enough supplies to feed 30,000 men for three months. Cargo ships brought cheese from Sardinia, rice and beans from Italy, wine from Crete.

The Armada gathered in Lisbon, Portugal. Medina Sidonia's 48-gun flagship, *San Martin*, led 130 ships. About half were fighting galleons and merchant ships. The rest were slow storeships, called hulks, and smaller vessels. Two hospital ships were ready for the wounded. Four galleasses, each with 50 guns, could be rowed on windless days, when sailing ships could not move. Galleys would row close to the beach to protect soldiers as they landed.

Spanish officers knew that the English had good ships, with many guns. So they brought extra guns and ammunition. With the fleet travelled 180 friars, to restore England to the Catholic faith. Many ships had saints' names and crosses on their sails.

△ **The Duke of Medina Sidonia** was 38 years old at the time of the Armada. He knew little of ships and was gloomy about the Armada's chances of success. But he was brave and loyal to both King Philip and Spain, and his high rank meant that he would be obeyed by his squadron commanders, all experienced seamen.

▽ **A Spanish two-wheeled land gun.** It was awkward to move and reload. Armada cannon fired a mix of ammunition. The fleet took 2,500 cannon, 124,000 cannon balls and half a million bullets, 7,000 hand-guns, 6,000 grenades, 11,000 pikes and 12 siege guns.

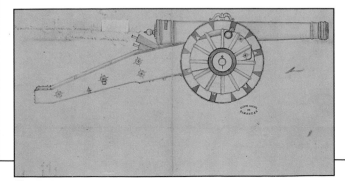

▷ **A Spanish soldier with a musket.** More than half the Armada's men were soldiers, trained to fight at sea. Each galleon had about 120 soldiers, 80 sailors and 50 gunners. The Spanish fired cannon at enemy ships from close range, then the soldiers boarded them. Squads of eight or ten men shared food rations.

◁ **An Armada galleon being loaded** with food, stores, cannon and war equipment for use in England. The fleet had ships from Portugal, Croatia, Italy, Germany and Poland, as well as from Spain.

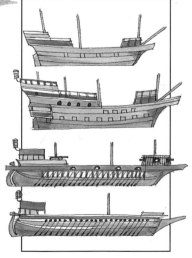

▷ **The Armada ships** included (top to bottom): merchant ships, galleons, galleasses (with sails and oars), and galleys (with oars only). Galleons were faster than merchant ships. Galleasses were slow, but heavily armed. Rough seas forced the Armada's four galleys to turn back.

On 30 May 1588, the Armada put to sea. It made slow progress and much of the food on the ships started to rot. Battered by storm winds, the fleet sailed back to Spain for repairs and fresh stores.

On 21 July the Armada set sail again, and four days later Medina Sidonia sent a message to Parma in the Netherlands. He told him to gather his forces for the invasion and to reply when he was ready to cross the Channel. The Armada was about to enter English waters.

THE ENGLISH NAVY

The English knew that the Spanish were coming and prepared to meet them. They planned to beat the Armada at sea, before Parma could land his army. The English would be fighting in ships that were faster and better armed than the Spanish.

▷ **Almost all the crew of an English ship were sailors.** Each man was trained to work the ship, heaving on ropes to raise and lower the sails.

The English had 197 ships – 66 more than the Armada – and their crews knew the Channel waters well. But they had fewer men (about 16,000), and a long coastline to defend. Many English ships were too small to hurt the Spanish fleet, but the newest English galleons were the best fighting ships of the day.

The English ships were crewed by sailors, with very few soldiers. Their captains planned to fight from a distance, move in to fire their cannon, and then turn away. They would avoid hand-to-hand fights on deck with Spanish soldiers, unless a Spanish ship was so damaged that it was easy to capture. An enemy ship taken as a 'prize' meant money for the victorious captain and crew. It was more valuable than an enemy ship sunk.

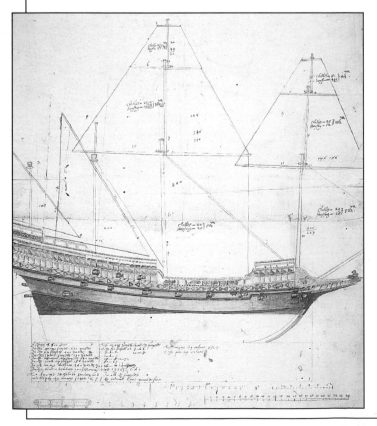

◁ **An English shipwright (builder) plans a new galleon** (top). The drawing (left) was probably made in 1586 by Matthew Baker, a shipwright. It shows an English galleon, with guns pointing through ports or openings. The raised front (forecastle) and rear (sterncastle) were lower than those of Spanish galleons.

> **Lord Howard of Effingham commanded the English fleet.**
> ● He was a cousin of Queen Elizabeth.
> ● He owned seven ships.
> ● He demanded extra stores and cannon balls, despite government complaints about cost.
> ● His officers were used to life at sea, unlike many Spanish nobles aboard the Armada.
> ● Howard was a land-fighter, but learned from his captains.

Henry VIII had built England's royal navy. Although about a third of its ships were new, some were 40 years old. The fleet was led by Lord Howard of Effingham. As well as warships, he commanded armed merchant ships and smaller coastal craft.

In Francis Drake, John Hawkins and Martin Frobisher, the English had captains who had often fought Spaniards before. Many English were scornful of the enemy: "Their ships are kept foul and beastly", one wrote. Yet, English ships sometimes strayed far off course, and crews became too drunk to fight. The Spanish were disciplined, good seamen, and had good maps. They would be hard to stop. On 29 July, the English had their first sight of the Armada as it sailed towards Plymouth.

> **English gunners practise** as they await the Armada. They were trained to fire and reload swiftly, moving the heavy guns on four-wheel trucks. Drake's ship had 24 gunners, 150 sailors and 76 soldiers. Crews slept on the decks. They ate meat, fish, cheese, and drank beer.

THE ARMADA APPROACHES

The first Englishmen to see the Armada were the crew of a Cornish ship making for France to collect a cargo of salt. Off the Scilly Isles they saw "nine sails of great ships, their sails all crossed over with a red cross". The Armada was advancing into the Channel.

News of the Armada spread rapidly. Small English ships sped into Cornish and Devon harbours, with more sightings of 'great ships'. Protestant preachers told people that the Spanish would use horrible tortures to force them to become Catholics, and would brand children with red-hot irons.

△ **On land, England's defences were ready.** This picture shows cannon and soldiers on the coast, and hilltop beacons being lit.

▷ **A map drawn by English shipbuilder Robert Adams after the battles** shows the Armada sailing into the Channel on 29 July.
● Two scout-ships, one Spanish, the other English, are shown.
● Some Armada captains wanted to attack Plymouth to capture a port where their ships could anchor.
● Medina Sidonia ordered the Armada to sail on and await the enemy's first move.

By dawn on 30 July the Spanish could see smoke rising from the beacons lit along the English coast. Medina Sidonia was wary. He had no port in which to anchor his fleet and no news of Parma's army. One of his scout-ships captured an English fishing boat. Its crew of four fishermen became the Armada's first prisoners. They told the Spanish of the English fleet that was preparing to attack.

▷ **The captured fishermen** (far right) told the Spanish to expect battle. The Armada moved into crescent-shaped fighting formation, spreading out over a distance of 3 kilometres. The commander and storeships were in the centre of the crescent.

The wind driving the Armada up the Channel was blowing against the English, yet many of their ships left Plymouth. That night, part of Lord Howard's fleet sailed across the Armada's front, while the rest slipped past it inshore. Now the English had the wind behind them and prepared for the first battle.

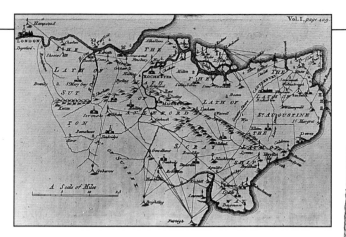

The Spanish fleet was organized in squadrons, each with ten or more fighting ships.
● Medina Sidonia in the *San Martin* led a group of Portuguese galleons.
● The slow storeships, or hulks, made up a separate squadron.

The English were led by Lord Howard in the *Ark Royal*.
● The biggest ship was Frobisher's *Triumph*, an old ship of 1,100 tonnes.
● Drake's 500-tonne *Revenge* was new and faster. Many ships were small.

△ **Blazing beacons warned people in England that the Armada was near.** This map of Kent drawn in 1585 shows the network of beacons set up on hills across southern England. Watchmen waited for a distant beacon to blaze, then lit their own fire to pass on the signal.

THE FIRST BATTLES

"The English had the advantage by reason of good gunpowder, good ships... and wind", said a Spanish soldier. On the morning of 31 July, the Armada captains saw the English fleet coming at them from behind.

▷ **The *San Salvador*** explodes. Half of its 400 men burned to death or jumped into the sea and drowned. Hawkins had the ship towed away as a prize.

In the first battles the English kept so far out of range that their guns did little damage.
● After the battle of Plymouth, however, the Armada lost two ships.
● The *San Salvador* blew up suddenly.
● The *Rosario* lost a mast in a collision, and was captured by Drake.
● After Plymouth, the Armada changed shape to a round mass. It no longer had trailing 'wings', easy to attack.

△ **This map by Robert Adams** shows how the English fleet (left) moved out of Plymouth to attack the Armada. The *Disdain* is firing the first shot.

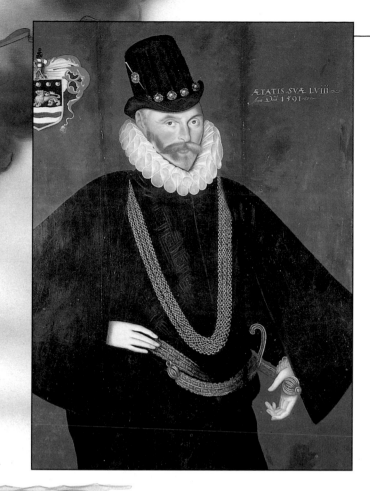

ÆTATIS SVÆ LVIII
Ano Dni 1591

△ **John Hawkins** was one of Howard's three squadron commanders. He had been on voyages with Francis Drake, and had modernized the English navy. Drake was already a knight. Hawkins and Frobisher were knighted during the Armada battles.

The English ships sailed one behind the other. This new tactic gave every ship in turn the chance to fire at the enemy. The Spanish were taken by surprise, but kept formation and sailed on.

The first battle, off Plymouth, was a skirmish. Two more fights followed. On 2 August off Portland Bill the Spanish galleasses almost caught Frobisher's squadron (group of ships), but were too slow. There was furious gunfire, but little damage done by either side.

The Armada sailed on. Unable to "pluck off the feathers" of this determined enemy, Howard split the English fleet into four roving squadrons. On 4 August the battle moved to the Isle of Wight. The wind dropped and ships had to be towed by rowing boats. When the wind freshened, English ships easily out-ran the Spanish.

The Armada could have anchored near the Isle of Wight, to wait for news of Parma. But the wind and the English attacks pushed the Spanish eastwards. The English broke off the fight to take on fresh food, water and ammunition. On 6 August the Armada reached Calais in France, still undefeated.

King ♣

The English Fleet whereof the L? Charles Howard was L? Admirall & S? Fran: Drake vice Admirall.

▷ **At the battle of Plymouth** (right), Spanish and English ships (shown above, on a 17th-century playing card) only exchanged fire. England was not officially at war with Spain.

FIRESHIPS!

"They came towards us all in flames, burning furiously..." This is how a Spaniard aboard the Armada remembered the fireship attack off Calais. Fire was a terrible danger to wooden ships packed with gunpowder and stores. The Armada was forced to scatter.

◁ **This illustration shows the fireship attack.** Six blazing ships drifted on the westerly wind and high tide. No Armada ship was burned, but the fleet scattered.

▽ **The battle** following the fireship attack.

△ **Fire-pots were deadly weapons** against wooden ships. Filled with flaming tar or oil and hurled at ships, they could destroy more quickly than cannon balls, which only broke ships' timbers.

France was not at war with Spain so the governor of Calais let the Armada anchor offshore, and buy fresh food and water. Small boats scurried from the town to the ships. Then a message came from Parma: Barges were gathered on the Dutch canals, but all the troops were not yet on board. The invasion of England could not begin for at least a week.

This was bad news for the Armada since it had no port to shelter in. The English fleet had the wind in its favour, and had been joined by more ships led by Sir Henry Seymour. Beyond Calais were the treacherous sandbanks of Flanders. There the ships of the Protestant Dutch waited in the shallows, ready to pounce on Parma's barges.

English and Spanish diplomats were still holding peace talks near Dunkirk as the Armada anchored off the French coast. Surprised, and seeing its fleet ready for battle, the English left the meeting hurriedly.

Out at sea, Howard decided to attack the Armada with fireships. Eight ships were packed with rags, timber and oil. With guns loaded, they were sent on the tide towards Calais.

◁ △ **The fireship attack was terrifying**, as these officers, in the cabin of a Spanish galleon (left), saw. The fireships, shown in the painting (above) of 1605, were crewed by volunteers. They got away in rowing boats before the blazing ships drifted in among the Spanish. The playing card (right) shows an Armada galleon raising its anchor to escape.

II ♣

The Spaniards on sight of the Fireships weighing Ancors cutting Cables and betaking themselves to flight to a hideous noise & in great Confusion.

The Armada's guard ships were on watch, and two fireships were towed out of harm's way. Crews quickly cut anchors free and moved their ships clear of danger. As the Armada scattered, the English moved in to attack. But Howard turned his squadron aside to seize a galleass stranded on shore, and this gave the Armada's best fighting ships time to regroup, ready for battle.

BATTLE OF GRAVELINES

"Unless we can find a harbour, we will perish", Medina Sidonia wrote to Parma on 7 August, the day before the English attacked the Armada. Between Gravelines (France) and Ostend (in what is now Belgium), the two fleets fought for nine hours at close range.

The ships came so close that their crews were able to exchange musket shots. Cannon roared. Black smoke from burning gunpowder clouded the air. Few men could see the enemy clearly. The Spanish soldiers were desperate to board the English ships and fight on deck. But the English held off, pouring gunfire into the enemy galleons until they had no more ammunition. The Armada's own guns did little damage.

◁ **The English win the final battle.** Small Dutch ships had patrolled the coast of the Low Countries. The Dutch Protestants had kept the Spanish invasion army in port, unable to help the Armada.

◁ **This painting shows Queen Elizabeth at Tilbury, after the battle.** There she made a stirring speech to her soldiers, awaiting the invasion. The Armada was not destroyed, as the picture suggests, but it was safe for the queen to visit her troops.

◁ ▽ **The battle of Gravelines.** The Spanish ship *Maria Juan* is sinking (top left in the painting). As shot crashed into the wooden ships, divers tried to patch up holes. Cannon balls took off men's limbs and heads. Bullets whined about the decks. An English gentleman had his bed shot from under him. A little later, a friend had his toes shot away.

The Spanish fought doggedly, struggling to help damaged ships and rescue shipmates from the waves. Not one ship surrendered to the English and only one Spanish merchant vessel was sunk. Two damaged galleons were captured by the Dutch. But about 1,000 of the Armada's men were killed and almost as many were wounded.

All day the Spanish were driven nearer the shore. By the afternoon, English guns were falling silent, but they had won the battle. Changing weather saved the Armada from the sandbanks and the waiting Dutch. The wind shifted, and by dawn next day the Spanish ships were safe in deep water. But they were in disorder, being blown away from all hope of joining with Parma's army. The Armada had failed.

▽ **Spanish ammunition**, ranging from cannon balls to lead shot for hand guns. These were recovered from an Armada wreck off Ireland. Unlike the English, the Spanish did not use up all their shot.

The Spanish fired their big guns too slowly. Gunners expected to fire one shot, then leave their cannon to fight on the deck of an enemy ship. They were not trained in rapid reloading of cannon.

STORM AND WRECK

While Elizabeth was speaking to her soldiers on 18 August, the Armada was sailing around Scotland. The wind had blown the fleet away into the North Sea. Its long journey home became a tragic test of seamanship and courage. The English rejoiced.

As the wind drove the Armada northwards, all its captains were in favour of turning back to fight again as soon as they could. Parma was at last loading his army into the barges. There was still a chance of invading England. But the wind did not ease. The English ships followed the Armada as far as Scotland, then turned triumphantly for home.

The Spanish faced a five-week voyage, around Scotland and then south round Ireland into the Atlantic Ocean. To guide them, they had maps, and captured Scots seamen as navigators. Supplies of food and drink were low, but given fair weather, all would still be well.

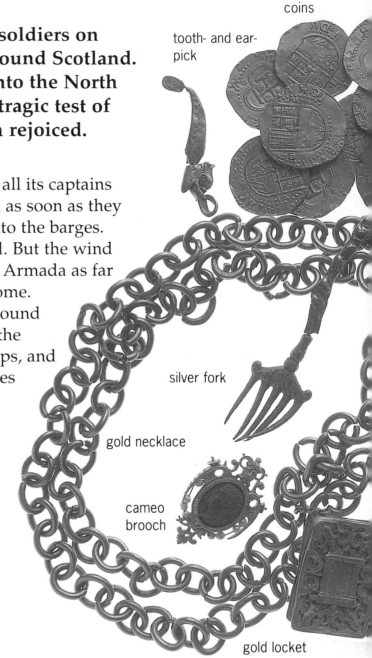

coins

tooth- and ear-pick

silver fork

gold necklace

cameo brooch

gold locket

△ **Queen Elizabeth's 'Armada portrait'.** The Queen who told her army at Tilbury, "I have the heart and stomach of a king", ruled England until 1603. On her death, Scotland's James VI, son of Mary, Queen of Scots, also became King James I of England.

▷ **The sites of Armada wrecks** dotted along the north and west coasts of Ireland. Other ships were wrecked off Scotland, or went down in the North Sea and the Atlantic Ocean. A few Spanish survivors were still in Ireland eight years after the Armada.

Armada wrecks off Ireland

IRELAND

◁ **Divers have brought up many objects from Armada wrecks** off the Irish coast. They have found gold and silver coins, gold chains and personal items (left). The wheel (below) is from a siege gun meant for Parma's army.

gold chain

▽ **The wreck of an Armada storeship** in the Shetlands. Most of this crew struggled ashore, reached Scotland, and got back to Spain.

Instead, the weather was foul, with rain, fog and bitter cold. Hurricane-force winds raised huge seas. Damaged ships lagged behind. Crews were sick, and food and water almost gone. Reports began reaching England of ships battling storms off Ireland. Ships which had lost anchors in the fireship attack could not be kept from smashing on to rocky shores. Many men drowned. Some struggled ashore to be killed by Irish looters or English troops. Lucky survivors were treated kindly or taken prisoner. Bands of Spaniards roamed Ireland, before escaping by ship.

Medina Sidonia got his flagship back to Spain on 21 September. Only 60 other ships were known to be safe. And 15,000 men never returned.

THE AFTERMATH

"No one could describe the misfortunes and miseries that have befallen us", wrote Medina Sidonia after the Armada. Bad planning, bad weather and bad luck had all led to failure. England was triumphant. Spain was shocked, but not beaten. The war went on.

▽ **Sir Francis Drake's drum** at Buckland Abbey in Devon. After the Armada, Howard, Drake and Hawkins set up a fund to help the wounded English sailors.

For Spain, the Armada was a disaster. Some people blamed the king, who never got over his disappointment. New ships were built, with better guns, and Spain sent other fleets against England in 1596 and 1597, but these, too, were beaten by storms.

The Dutch, like the English, raided Spain's empire in America, and won their freedom from Spanish rule, though not until 1648. As Spain's power weakened slowly, England started to build its own overseas empire. Had the Armada joined forces with Parma, and Parma landed his army in Kent, it might have been a different story.

▷ **England and Spain finally made peace** in 1604. This is a painting of the peace talks in London. Among the English (right) was Lord Howard of Effingham, seated second from the window.
● Elizabeth died in 1603, so James I was now king of England.
● Philip II of Spain had died in 1598.
● Hawkins and Drake died of sickness in the Caribbean, fighting the Spanish in 1595-96.

GLOSSARY

admiral commander of a fleet.

allies people or countries working or fighting together

ambassador a country's representative in a foreign land.

ammunition shot fired from guns, such as lead balls or rounded stones.

arquebus early hand-gun, larger than a musket.

artillery big guns used on ships or on land.

beacons fires lit on hills or towers as warnings or guides to ships at sea.

bows front end of a ship.

broadside shots fired by all the guns along one side of a ship.

cannon big gun, often mounted on a carriage.

castle land fortress; also a raised platform on an old-fashioned warship.

chart map of ocean and coasts used by sailors.

diplomat government official who deals with foreign countries.

exile a person being sent away from their homeland.

friars religious teachers and preachers.

galleass warship with oars and sails.

galleon sailing warship, less top-heavy than older ships.

galley long, low warship driven by oars, useful in calm, shallow waters.

heresy an idea or belief, usually about religion, that is against accepted teachings.

hulk slow cargo ship.

Inquisition organization in the Roman Catholic Church for seeking out heresy.

Low Countries lands now known as Belgium and the Netherlands.

musket early hand-gun, like a long rifle.

noble aristocrat or landowner, with a title, such as a duke.

pike soldier's weapon, like an axe on a long pole.

stern back end of a ship.

trained bands volunteer soldiers.

Map of western Europe in 1588, showing the Armada's route. The Armada sailed from Lisbon (Portugal), but had to regroup in Corunna in northern Spain. Then it crossed the Bay of Biscay to enter the English Channel. The main battles took place between Plymouth and the Isle of Wight, and off the coast of Flanders (modern Belgium). The Duke of Parma's army was in the Spanish Netherlands. After Gravelines, the Armada sailed round Scotland and Ireland. The survivors returned to Spain.

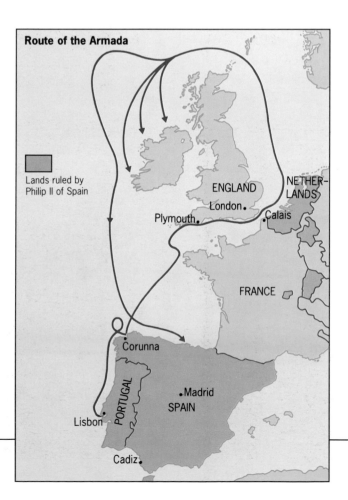

Route of the Armada

Lands ruled by Philip II of Spain

ENGLAND
London
Plymouth
Calais
NETHER-LANDS
FRANCE
Corunna
PORTUGAL
Madrid
SPAIN
Lisbon
Cadiz

23

INDEX